OLD RHONDDA

in photographs

(*overleaf*): **1** The Old Fulling Mill, Tonypandy, from which the name of the town is derived. It was operated from 1738 until the latter part of the nineteenth century. An unsuccessful attempt was made to transfer the loom and wheel to the National Museum of Wales in 1914.

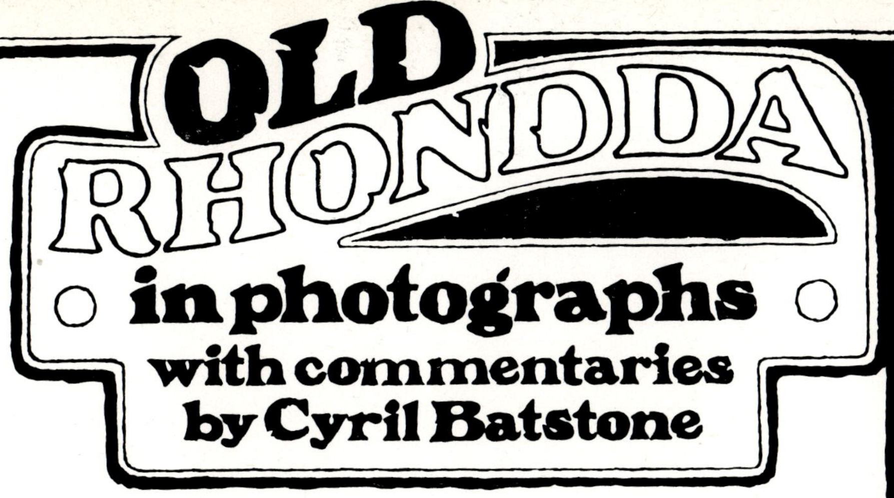

OLD RHONDDA

in photographs

with commentaries by Cyril Batstone

FOREWORD BY GWYN THOMAS

STEWART WILLIAMS, PUBLISHERS

BRYN AWEL, BUTTRILLS ROAD, BARRY, GLAMORGAN

First published July 1974
Second impression July 1974
Third impression June 1975
© Stewart Williams, Publishers
ISBN 0 900807 08 3

Printed in Wales by
D. BROWN AND SONS LIMITED
COWBRIDGE AND BRIDGEND, GLAMORGAN

PROCESS ENGRAVING BY CARDIFF PHOTO ENGRAVERS LTD
PORTMANMOOR ROAD, SPLOTT, CARDIFF

BOUND BY WESTERN BOOK CO. LIMITED, MAESTEG

Contents

Foreword

by Gwyn Thomas

the celebrated author, playwright and television personality

IN THIS BOOK you will find a living map, a vivid evocation, of one of the world's most astonishing and inspiring places.

For the last hundred years the Rhondda Valley has been one of Britain's darker marvels. It is made up of two deep gulches in the North Glamorgan hills. Between 1870 and 1920 it poured out enough coal to have coked the globe if ignited at one stroke. Pit shafts opened like the holes in a mature cheese. Never was a small stretch of earth so majestically ransacked.

And the people who lived between the Rhondda hills were infinitely more interesting and precious than the stuff they hauled out of the rich seams and exported to any part of the earth in need of power. Singularly little of the wealth they produced stuck to the valley people's fingers. They generated a unique humour, fortitude and goodness, a currency not recognised at the bank.

They worked, worshipped, sang and laughed at record levels. It was a place gifted and deprived, glorious and absurd, in equal measure. The Rhondda was conjured out of a sweet solitude of which a few green, gracious remnants can still be seen.

It was created by a world mad for steam, warmth and money. In a few decades it had achieved a city-sized population. In just two decades between the wars the great army of folk who had poured into the valley from every part of the British compass had slipped away. Pits closed like flies' eyes. Coal tumbled from its throne and in the Rhondda's heart was felt not a single, republican regret. Diminished somewhat from its noonday prime but still packing a huge human wallop, it remains a fascinating episode in humanity's long trek in search of a final security.

The pictures that follow, preserved by golden luck, add up to a portrait of this remarkable place. The story is all here.

Look at the details of transport. Movement was important to the valley. Life could, of an instant, become threatening, claustrophobic, and the odd outing was a glittering event. I saw many memorable journeys in these awful, unsprung charabancs. In the days when the automobile was even less trusted than it is now, the pioneer travellers, the charanauts, would take their places on the wooden benches, tense as men being bounced off to the moon.

All-men outings on the charabancs were regarded as occasions of daring and debauchery. In the randier sections of the glens lots would be drawn to decide which of the argonauts would remain sober to load the others back into the vehicle at the end of the beery day.

But the trams were the high-spot. Trams in areas like Birmingham which are reasonably flat are tolerable. But the Rhondda was a place of cracking slopes and the trams were narrow contraptions that developed an almost rubbery wobble when they went crashing down the worse gradients.

It was rumoured that one could be flung out of the tram if one's seat happened to be on the open roof, and it was claimed that along the more hazardous descents where the trams made their most mischievous lurches, buildings were equipped with springs that shot the flying passengers back into the same tram if not the same seat.

A preacher once travelled from Maerdy to Ynyshir, an Alpine run if ever there was one, to give a sermon. He rode on a tram that for some reason got out of control. The tram exhausted its devilry on the flat stretch on the south side of Wattstown. The minister was helped out, ashen with dismay. He had apparently been in the middle of some profound thought about man's fiendishness, when the tram broke free from any human agency and started to career towards Wattstown like a heavy rock flung over a cliff. The preacher stood in the pulpit for twenty minutes and did not speak a word. The audience, thinking religion had at last given up the ghost, asked the deacons to send a request to the preacher that he break the news one way or the other.

The minister walked down the pulpit steps without opening his mouth. He had decided that Rhondda trams could not be placed in the context of a redeemable species. He retired to his native village in Cardiganshire where he put a rigid ban on electricity and wheels.

Consider the housing patterns revealed in some of these photographs. Ideally the Rhondda would have provided pleasant accommodation for about ten thousand people. At its peak, 200,000 immigrants found homes there. The great hollow filled to the brim. The long terraces ascended further and further up the slopes. Some of the side-streets rose almost straight from the valley-bed. Shoppers from the top terraces, after too abrupt a canter down to the shopping area, often suffered mild shock and had to be slapped or fed with hot tea before they were able to remember the object of their errand.

Older people, stuck up on the heights, especially if tortured by rheumatism, one of the valley's prime curses, would give up the challenge of toiling up and down, anchor themselves permanently to their kitchens and keep in random touch by shout or semaphore.

The opening of bus routes over the most forbidding ridges, Porth to Tonypandy, Ton Pentre to Ferndale, had a social impact as dramatic as the opening of America's Union Pacific but with less trouble from Indians. The older generation at the time the buses came regarded every Rhondda citizen using transport for any journey less than ten miles as effete or perverted. The effect of climbing hills on bones made weak by a poor diet could be sinister. Many a lad by the age of ten could be bow-legged enough to be rolled by a skilled hand.

The builders of the Rhondda must have had a nightmare of a time. Streets built on capricious hillsides look like bucking broncos shooting off course at wildly erratic angles. The builders found areas of peat which failed to provide a sure foundation.

Houses built in questionable areas could be rented only to the light-weight type of tenant or they and the property would sink into the loam.

On top of this the vast web of underground workings kept the top-soil twitching as a drug addict, and houses originally built as two up, two down, became none up and four down. One of the problems facing local hospitals was getting incoming patients accustomed to flat beds. In my village a combination of loud singing and a drastic subsidence of the foundations brought a pub down in ruins and stopped drinking in its tracks so abruptly it kept the temperance reformers supplied with pamphlet material for years to come.

The shops, of which, in their bulging comprehensiveness, the photographs give us some marvellous examples, were a special feature of the Rhondda. They always reminded me of the stores in an American frontier town. Community centres in miniature, higgledy-piggledy piles of treasure in which the restless young found it easy to get lodged and lost. A half-hour before closing time a thorough sweep-through was made for missing persons.

Shop-lifting in the less Calvinistic districts must have become something of an art-form and several of the more distraught traders put the departing customers on the scales and charged them, not on individual items but on their total weight.

In the lean years many shopkeepers showed an heroic comradeship with their needy customers and went irretrievably through the hoop because of it. The place was full of an oxygen of sharing and caring. If all the lights of the world were put out you could still see the Rhondda glow bright and consoling in the dark.

The chip shops and Italian cafés were the heart of our night life. In my local chip-shop I was hoisted nightly on to a lemonade box and made to sing for the waiting customers. As a reward I was fed with endless bags of "scrumps", fragments of batter made to smart with salt and swim in vinegar. My family had to rescue me when I showed signs of a chipped larynx and advanced carbohydrate poisoning, batter-fatigue.

The photographs give us a clear image of what ran coal neck and neck as the valley's masterwork. If the physical presence of piety, the stones of the temples, could guarantee a better quality of mankind, then the people of the Rhondda would long ago have been paying rates and taxes adjusted to the needs and rewards of angels. Never was there such a violence of singing hope. The valley was one continuous chapel. Fine optimistic Sundays were one massive harp of exultation. From my home I was within shouting distance of seven chapels and I served at odd times as a chorister in every one of them to qualify for the annual treat to the seaside.

There was nothing fancy about the face of the chapels. They had a square, utilitarian look, as if they were telling salvation that time was short and to get a move on. The great wave of prayer and singing has ebbed now. Most of the chapels now wear an air of shoddy dereliction. But in the days we see in these photographs, every chapel was a great fortress of expectancy, powered by a rage against injustice and the hope of a decent peace among the peoples of the earth. To anyone treated to a childhood in a robust Rhondda chapel congregation, any evidence of continued vileness brings in a shudder of shocked disbelief. We really believed, after the dozenth rendering of "Calon Lân" or "Cwm Rhondda" in belting harmony and with a good acoustic in the chapel gallery, that Satan had at last been given his cards and shown the door.

Even today, pass a chapel in which that unique passion once surged and you will feel the air moved by a vibration that will not cease as long as men and women still have their being between Treherbert and Maerdy in the north to Porth in the south.

Disaster ripped great holes in the life of the Rhondda. Collieries and legions of admirable men died when explosion, flood and fire tore through the tunnels. One of the most remarkable pictures in this book shows the rescuers and survivors of the Tynewydd cataclysm of a hundred years ago. Misfortune could rampage on broad fronts. Methane and water had a thousand ways of going mad below ground. We knew men who had survived the ordeal of entombment in the hungry dark and the shadow on their faces arched over our minds like a troubled sky. A memory of wounds hung in the air like the aftertaste of thunder.

The shock of losses that tore the heart out of small communities intensified the passion and poetry of comradeship. Everything about the valley seemed to do that. The closeness of the hills, the density of the streets that ran in grey streaks along the slopes, the dangers that could erupt in a few minutes on a calm afternoon and betray the peace and sanity of life for years to come, all these things, for me, are heard in the throbbing richness of the massed singing, the rhythm of the quick and ardent speech of the Rhondda people. Their total experience has been a moving sound of kindliness and courage, deepened by terrible echoes. Had the Rhondda evolved one great anthem to itself it would have been a unique salute to the cruelty and the greatness of life among the common folk. The Rhondda mind grew bright over the task of sorting the ecstasy from the outrage.

We set up, in our modest way, some kind of record. Never has so much talent been swilled down the waste-pipe of the world's contempt. Logically we should be sending in our unpaid bills to the world's treasurers until the end of time.

Watch out for the children's faces in these studies. Children of storms with the gentleness of lambs. I could spend hours staring at the picture of that feast of buns contributed by one of the local publicans. Looking at it and recalling a similar experience I could feel once again the grief of a stomach overborne by dough, the sticky caress of sugar around the fingers, and the cleansing touch of tears around the heart.

Gwyn Thomas

Introduction

THE RHONDDA VALLEYS occupy a unique place in the social history of Wales. Its people are all too familiar with extreme hardship and danger and they have known soul-destroying poverty which would have crushed lesser communities. From the shadows has emerged a closely-knit, courageous, warm-hearted people.

Some 190 photographs drawn from the superb collection built up by Cyril Batstone, who writes the commentaries, mirror Rhondda life—from everyday situations and places, to the traumatic effects of disaster—over a period of sixty years.

Cyril Batstone was born at Cwmparc in 1924. His eldest brother was killed in the Abergorki Colliery at the age of fifteen on his first day at work, while his father, a miner when there was work, died as a result of pneumoconiosis in 1940. But for these tragedies he might have followed them down the mines. Instead Cyril Batstone pursued various jobs in the electricity industry and spent four years in the R.A.F. before setting up in business as a photographer at Pentre in 1953.

He was elected a member of the Institute of British Photographers in 1954 and served as president of the South Wales and Monmouthshire Centre of the Institute in 1962-63. He is a founder member and at present a member of the committee of "Cymdeithas y Rhondda" (The Rhondda Society).

Cyril Batstone's interest in everything relating to the history of his beloved Rhondda is already well-known and the value of his pioneering work in collecting photographs of the area will increase immeasurably with the passage of time.

The value of the book is enhanced by the foreword which has been contributed by Gwyn Thomas, whose associations with the area and reputation as an author, playwright and television personality are recognised far beyond his native Wales.

The Illustrations

I REGARD IT as my good fortune that being a professional photographer with an insatiable appetite for local history I am in something of a unique position to help in the preservation of many fascinating and historically valuable prints which in less favourable circumstances might be lost or destroyed. Even so my interest would virtually be still-born without the generous and enthusiastic support of many friends throughout the Rhondda who have assisted me in the building of a collection which at present numbers 1,400 photographs.

Some of the retrieval stories behind these wonderful old prints are worth recording. Several were "preserved" under linoleum, one was used as a substitute for a broken pane of glass in the window frame of a railway hut, at least three arrived by courtesy of observant refuse collectors, while one of the most priceless—that of Dinas Middle Colliery in 1879—was saved in the nick of time from a bucket of hot ashes, with only minor scorching on the mount.

Every effort has been made to restore the prints to something resembling their original condition. Regrettably, hardly any of the old glass negatives have survived, so every print has had to be carefully copied and the best result obtained. It is a tantalising thought that there must still be countless old photographs hidden away from sight—and often unappreciated when eventually discovered. If this book succeeds in stimulating an interest in the history of the Rhondda Valleys it will have achieved its purpose and amply repaid me for many hours spent in the dark room.

Pentre,
Rhondda

Cyril Batstone

ACKNOWLEDGEMENTS

Many of the photographers whose work is featured in this book are unknown, but we are pleased to set down the names of those who have been traced and we gratefully record our indebtedness to Ernest T. Bush, Levi Ladd, Tonypandy, Lester of Treherbert, D. J. Ryan and Stephen Timothy of Pentre, and Albert Davies, Porth. The photographs of the miners rescued in the Tynewydd Colliery inundation of 1877 were taken by W. and D. Downey, London and Newcastle, at the special request of Queen Victoria.

In addition our thanks are extended to Dr. E. D. Lewis whose magnificent The Rhondda Valleys *has been an invaluable source of reference; Dr. Gerwyn Thomas, Assistant Keeper, Department of Industry, National Museum of Wales; Rhondda Borough Library; Cardiff Public Libraries; The Rhondda Society; Mr. Derek Clayton, Ton Pentre; and finally Miss Eileen Davies, Rhondda Borough Librarian, and Mr. Roy Denning, for reading the proofs and making a number of useful suggestions.*

Rural Rhondda

2 Ty ar y Twyn, Tonypandy, *c*.1895. This farm was situated on the hillside above the mill. Mrs. Powell and family, seen in the photograph, were the last occupants. Now the site of Tonypandy Public Library.

3 Ystradfechan House, Cwmparc, *c.*1900. This old Rhondda farm was later used as a residence by the General Manager of the Ocean Coal Co., Ltd.

4 Ty yn y Cymmer, overlooking Y Bont Fawr, Porth, *c.*1900. It was occupied in the early 1900s by the South Wales Bible Institute whose principal was the Rev. R. B. Jones.

7 Upper Cymmer Colliery (or Pwll Hindes), sunk in 1851. Water from this colliery broke through and flooded the neighbouring Tynewydd Colliery trapping 14 miners in April 1877.

8 Ystrad Brickworks, *c.*1880. One of the few non-colliery brickworks in the Rhondda. Price of bricks—3/- per 100. Taken from a badly stained and faded albumen print.

9 Bute Colliery, Cwmsaebren, Treherbert. The first steam coal colliery sunk in the Rhondda in 1851 by W. S. Clarke for the trustees of the Bute estate. The population of the parish of Ystradyfodwg was approximately 950 at this time.

10 Cymmer Colliery, Porth, *c.*1865. Scene of an explosion on 15 July 1856, in which 114 miners lost their lives and 42 were seriously injured.

11 Cymmer Colliery, Porth, 1910. A photograph taken at the pit-head shortly after a baulk of wood fell down the shaft trapping the cage and injuring a miner.

12 Farrier Harries Oxworth and his assistant, Tommy Walters, shoeing on top of No. 9 Colliery, Tylorstown, 1924.

13 Miners and surface workers on top of the Cambrian Colliery in 1880. Albumen print.

14 Glamorgan Colliery in full production, 1900. Shaft sunk to Rhondda No. 2 and 3 seams in March 1863. Fire clay from between these two seams was used to produce 10,000 bricks a day by the turn of the century, along with 1,400 tons of coke a week from 281 ovens.

15 Until the building of pit-head baths by the more enlightened coal-owners in the 1930s miners had to make do at home with a wooden tub or galvanised bath in front of the fire.

16 Ynysfeio Colliery, Ynyswen. Sunk by James Thomas of Ynyshir and his partners Mathew Cope (Cardiff) and John Lewis (Aberdare) in 1854.

17 Dare Colliery, Cwmparc, opened by David Davies in April, 1870. A dynamo for lighting the top of the colliery was installed in 1880.

18 Pay day at "Gorki" Colliery (Drift), Clydach Vale, *c*.1900.

19 Disused balance wheel near Nant Ffernol, Treherbert, *c*.1915. The wheel was used to haul up empty trams by the weight of the full journey descending the tram-road built to serve a coal level on the hillside.

20   Building of Tallis Street, Cwmparc, *c*.1890.

21 Arch of coal at the entrance to Glamorgan Colliery built for the visit to Tonypandy of the Prince and Princess Alexander of Teck, 24 April 1914.

Townships

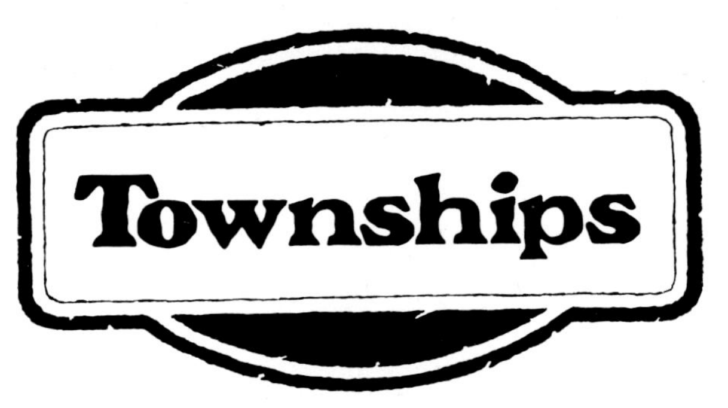

22 Zion Hill, Tonypandy, *c.*1920.

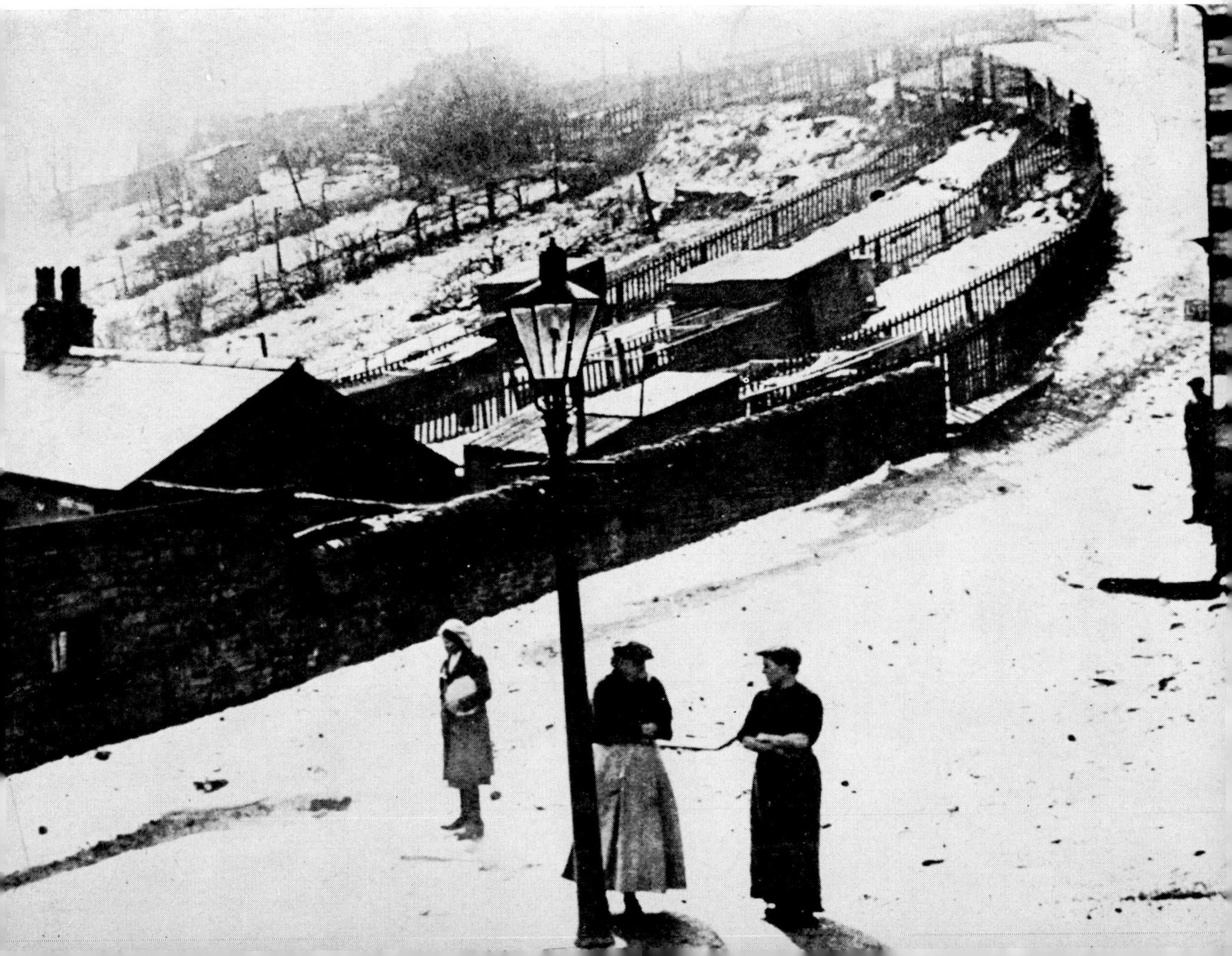

23 Tonypandy Square prior to the rebuilding of the Pandy Hotel, *c.*1900.

24 Tonypandy Square showing the original site of the horse trough and monument, *c.*1910.

25 Ystrad Road, Pentre, with main Post Office, Lories Outfitters and Pawnbroker on the right, 1910.

26 Golden Age, Williamstown, with the lines of the Ely and Clydach branch railway passing underneath the bridge *c*.1900.

27 Old White Rock Houses, Dinas Road, Penygraig. Until October 1879 the brook of Ffrwd Amos marked the boundary between the parishes of Llantrisant and Ystradyfodwg.

28 Bridgend Square, Pentre, in the 1930s after erection of Belisha Beacons (named after the then Transport Minister Hore Belisha).

29 Cymmer Road, Porth, with hay stores and carriage repair workshops on the right, 1901.

30 Darran Lake, Ferndale, *c.*1900. Now part of the pleasant Darran Public Park and Children's Playground.

31 Porth Square, taken from Cymmer Hill with "Y Bont Fawr" in foreground, *c.*1880. The large house in right centre was the home of Dr. Naunton Davies and is now the site of a Telephone Exchange (*see* **99**).

32 General view of Ferndale with the stacks of Ferndale No's 1 and 5 collieries in the foreground, and No's 2 and 4 in the far distance. The odd one out, Ferndale No. 3, was at Bodringallt in the Rhondda Fawr.

33 Parade of Rechabites near Rhondda Hotel, Ferndale. The road is in course of being rebuilt, *c.*1912.

34 Cardiff Arms Hotel, Treorchy, *c*.1910. Home of Treorchy Football Club. The open space in front was used as a site for a mini-market on Saturday nights.

35 High Street, Treorchy, from the Red Cow Hotel, near the site of Tynybedw Farm, *c*.1910.

36 High Street, Treorchy, with ice-cream and vinegar carts outside Bethlehem Chapel, *c*.1910. Tynybedw Colliery, sunk in 1876 by Edmund Thomas of Maindy Hall, is in the background.

37 Ynysfeio Bridge, Ynyswen. Widened in 1927. Completely removed and surrounding area landscaped in February 1972.

38 Road repairs 1904-style at High Street, Treorchy. All main roads on the Bute estate were made at least 50 ft. wide so that a coach and horses could turn in their width.

39 Footbridge, built in 1928, to enable inhabitants of Stanleytown to cross Tylorstown Colliery safely to the shopping centre of Tylorstown.

40 Stanleytown from Pontygwaith with Co-operative stores on the right. The Co-ops were strongly supported, paying a dividend on goods purchased.   Miners' families could draw upon money thus saved from their "black books" in times of need. The first Co-op was established at Treorchy in 1868.

41 Ystrad Road, Pentre. Photograph taken just before landslide in 1916.

42 Ynyshir with Standard Colliery in full production. Sunk by James Thomas, a former 3/- per day underground workman, in 1876.

43 Queen Square, Tylorstown, *c*.1914. The town was named after Alfred Tylor, a Londoner who started sinking his colliery on Pendyrys land in 1873.

44 Lower Dunraven Street, Tonypandy. The Methodist Church on the right was demolished and the Central Hall built on the site in 1923.

45 Wern Street, Clydach Vale, *c*.1900. The children are playing hook and wheel.

46 Berw Road, Tonypandy, *c.*1920.

47 A general view of Treorchy with Tylacoch Colliery on the right, now the site of a Comprehensive School, *c*.1900.

48 Bute Street, Treorchy, 1904, with Barmouth Temperance Bar on the right.

49 Road improvements at High Street, Treorchy, shortly before the National Eisteddfod in 1928.

50 Ystrad Library, opened in 1896 and destroyed by enemy bombing on the night of 29-30 April 1941.

51 Ystrad Road, Pentre, *c*.1900. This was the main shopping centre for the top end of Rhondda Fawr before the closure of Pentre Colliery when it was superseded by the better-situated Treorchy.

52 Tynewydd, Treherbert, with Tydraw Colliery in the middle distance and Tynewydd Farm lower left, *c*.1928.

53 Maerdy Railway Station, opened to passenger traffic 18 June 1889.

54 Cwmparc with hexagonal bandroom in Lower Terrace where the Park and Dare Silver Band (formerly Brass Temperance Band) used to practise. The band was formed in 1896.

55 Taff Street, Ferndale, on coal day. The concessionary coal was delivered outside the houses, later to be carried to the coal-house by the miners after finishing their day's work.

56 River bridge at the lower end of Elizabeth Street, Pentre, with visiting fair and boxing booth in background. These frail wooden bridges were frequently engulfed and sometimes swept away in times of flood.

57 Pontypridd Furniture Co. Shop, Dunraven Street, Tonypandy. On the upper floor was the Tonypandy and Trealaw Free Library, established by local businessmen in 1899, the first free library in the Rhondda.

58 Hannah Street, Porth, the shopping centre for lower Rhondda Fach and Fawr, *c.*1900. The headquarters of Thomas & Evans, the grocers, are prominent on the right.

59 General view of Tyntyla and Ystrad. The small building in the centre of the photograph is Ystradyfodwg Cottage Hospital, the first hospital in the Rhondda. Opened in 1887 with four beds, increased to ten in 1897 when the population of the Rhondda was about 100,000.

60 Cwmparc, with Parc Isaf Farm in the foreground, at the top end of Railway Terrace, the first houses built in Cwmparc following the sinking of Parc Colliery in 1865. The farm was then occupied by David Llewellyn, grandfather of Sir D. R. Llewellyn, Aberdare.

61   The Huts, Tonypandy, built in 1862 for Archibald Hood to house the sinkers of Glamorgan Colliery. Demolished in 1963 to make way for a modern block of flats named after Alderman Sydney Mitchell.

62   Appletree, Dinas, 1904, near the site of the first colliery sunk in the Rhondda by Walter Coffin of Bridgend, *c*.1815. Dinas was formerly called Castellau.

63 Tynewydd, Treherbert, with a multitude of coal-levels to the coal-outcrops on the hillside, opened by miners in times of depression and strikes.

64 Dunraven Street, Tonypandy, *c*.1908.

65 Ceridwen Street and Maerdy Road, Maerdy, *c*.1905.

66 Strand, Ferndale, *c*.1905. The original name, Glyn Rhedynog, was changed to Ferndale in the 1860s.

67 The first tram service in the Rhondda was opened between Trehafod and Partridge Road, Llwynypia, in July 1908. Two months later the line was extended to Treherbert.

68 Llwynypia Station (Taff Vale Railway), *c*.1895.

69   Maindy, Ton Pentre, winter 1939. Ton Co-operative Bakery on the left.

70   Pentre, with lower Cae Mawr before the erection of T. C. Jones and E.M.I. factories. The Pentwyn new road linking Ton Pentre with Cwmparc was built in the mid-1920s.

Bought of T. & J. RICHARDS,
(Late EDWARD SKYRME.)
Wholesale and Retail Grocers.
The Stores, Pentre, RHONDDA VALLEY.

71 Bill for food supplies for school party to celebrate Queen Victoria's Diamond Jubilee, 20 June 1897. The account was made out to W. Jenkins of Ystradfechan House.

72 Joe and Ivor Owens of Brynteg Bakery, Ystrad, *c*.1921. The business was founded by their mother in 1917 to provide her sons with an alternative to working underground.

73 Delivery cart of Sharpe Bros., Treorchy and Pentre, *c*.1910.

74   Watkins & Sons, Flannel Merchants, Tonypandy, *c*.1920.

75   Sharpe Brothers came to the Rhondda from Suffolk in 1900 and soon became one of the biggest fruit and vegetable merchants in the Upper Rhondda. Photograph taken *c*.1916.

SPRATT'S
PATENT
CHICKEN
MEAL
IN
SEALED
BAGS
The Morning Feed
SPRATT'S PATENT
DOG CAKES

SPRATT'S
CHIKKO
FOR CHICKS
Buy it in Sealed Bags

RODNIM
SPRATT'S
MEAL FOR DOGS
MELOX DOG FOOD
MELOX DOG FOOD
LIPTON'S TEA
IRONMONG
LIPTON'S TEA
SPRATTS CHIKKO FOR CHICKS
SPRATTS PATENT DOG CAKES
PICKS & BORING MACHINES
CONCERT

(opposite): **76** R. T. Jones, Ironmonger, Bute Street, Treherbert. Supplier of powder and detonators to local collieries

77 J. H. Powell, Milliner and Draper, Garfield House, Treherbert, *c*.1900.

78 Iorwerth & Thomas, Saddlers, Llewellyn Street, Pentre, 1895.

79 E. Dutfield, Draper, Outfitter, General Dealer and Post Office, Penyrenglyn, Treherbert, *c.*1900.

80 International Stores, Bridgend Square, Pentre, 1905.

81 The Calcutta Tea Stores, Pentre, displaying goods for redemption of stamps collected from tea packets, *c*.1910.

82 Richard Thomas, Picture Framer and Glazier, with family, Bute Street, Treorchy, 1910.

PEGLERS
PURITAN SOAP
CHECKMATE CARBOLIC SOAP
PURITAN SOAP
PEC

(*opposite*): **83** Pegler's Stores, Pentre, one of six chain stores and two Co-ops which thrived in Pentre during the boom days.

84 Heavy-duty haulage cart, Ynysynon Road, Trealaw, *c*.1920.

85 Evan Edwards delivering milk to 23 Parc Road, Cwmparc, 1930.

86 A. Canale, ice cream vendor, Parc Road, Cwmparc, 1924. Immigrants from Northern Italy arrived in 1890 and opened coffee-shops which soon became convivial meeting-places. All were affectionately called "Bracchi" shops after the first immigrants.

87   Briggs & Company, Pentre, *c*.1910. The price of footwear ranged from 3/6d to 12/6d.

88   Studleys Fruit Shop, Tonypandy Square. Founded 1890.

89 Female Conductors were employed during the First World War because of the shortage of labour. This photograph was taken in 1915.

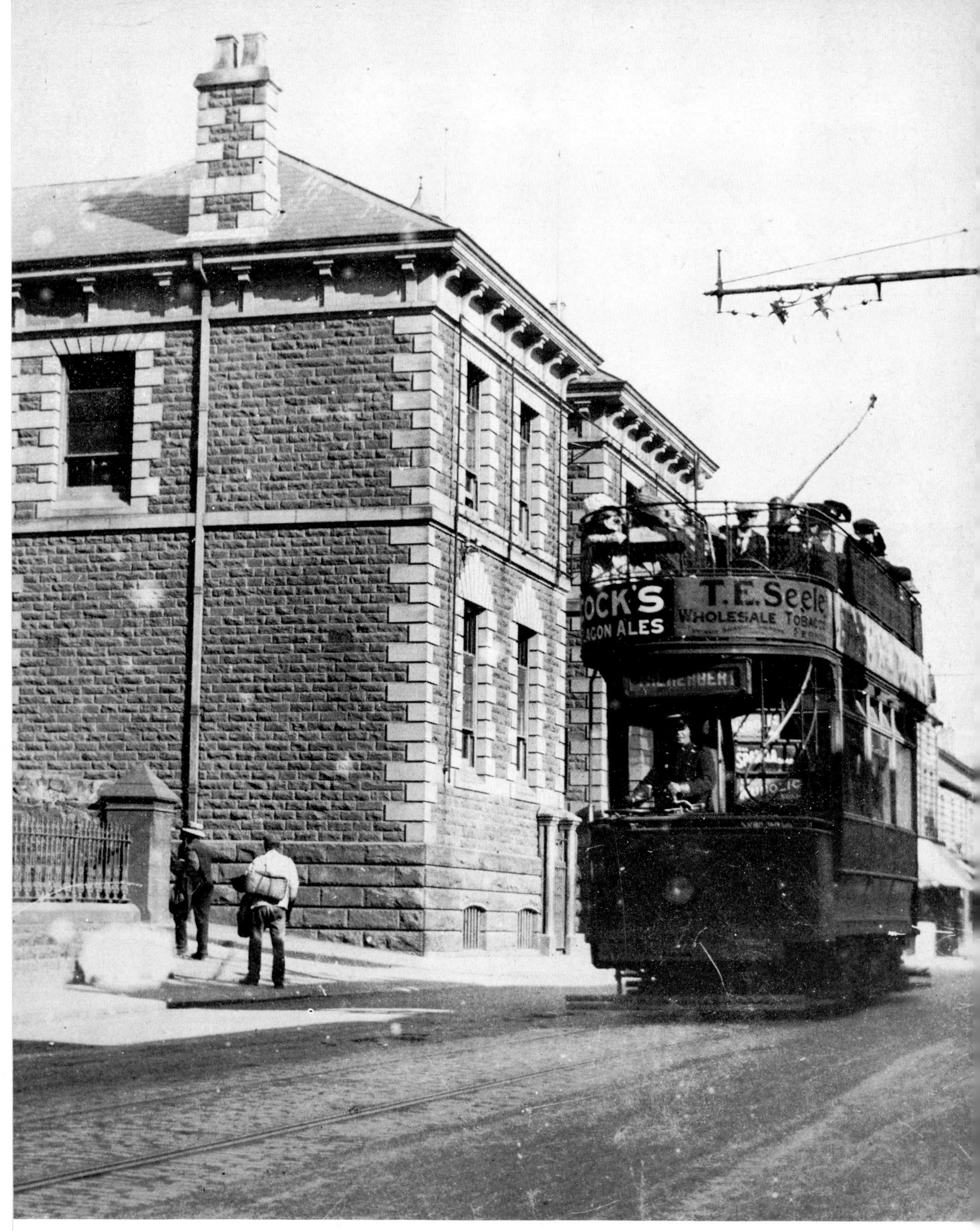

94 Open-topped tram passing the Council Offices, Pentre. The offices were built in 1882 and at the time the foreman builder was paid 6d. per hour and craftsmen masons 4d. per hour. The Pennant sandstone was dressed by hand on the site.

95 Motor coach tour, 1926. Pneumatic tyres and improved roads made a charabanc journey rather more comfortable than in solid-tyre days.

96 Every tram carried a fleet number and raffles were held in some parts of the valleys to determine what number tram would pass a selected point at a given time, for example the first tram to pass the Stag Hotel, Treorchy, on Sunday morning.

97   Brewery dray converted with hard benches for employees' outing, Ferndale, *c*.1920.

98   "Lily of the Valley" charabanc with operator, R. T. George, Pentre Foundry owner, outside the Bridgend Hotel, Pentre, *c*.1920.

99 Porth Square, July 1933, with one of the first 'buses used on general service. The last tram was withdrawn on 1 February 1934 (*see 31*).

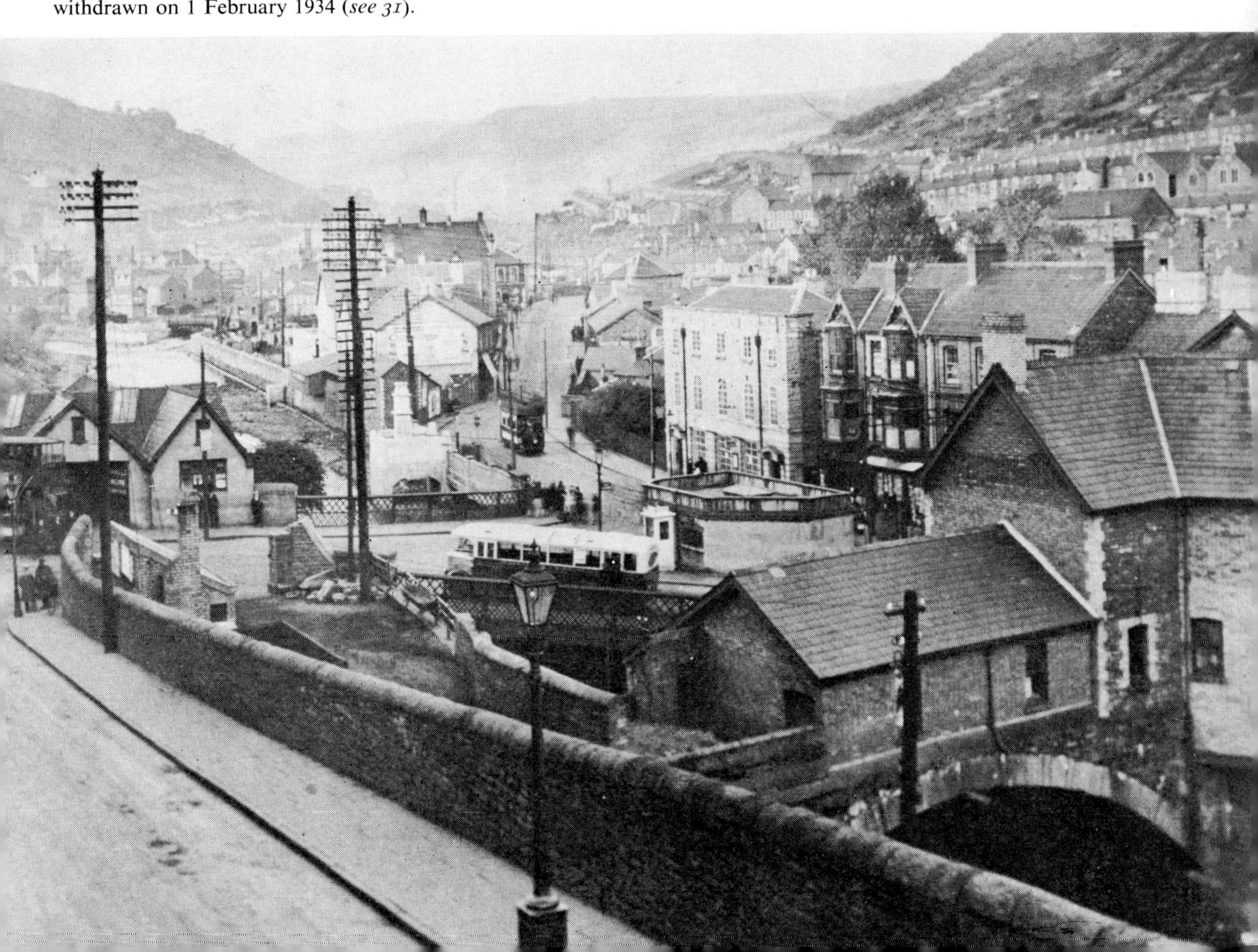

100 Tynycymmer Hill, Dinas, *c*.1900. Cabs (as seen in this photograph) and brakes were the principal means of transport between railway stations.

101 Rhondda Tramways Company 'bus as used on service to Clydach Vale, August 1920.

102   The entrance to the Rhondda Transport Bus Depot, Tynewydd Square, Porth, decorated for the Coronation celebrations of King George VI and Queen Elizabeth, 1937.

103 Steam lorry used for the collection of refuse from bunker depots and its transportation to the destructor plant at Porth, *c*.1922.

104 Chain-drive van used as Army transport in First World War and converted to peace-time use by Nicholas Coachbuilders, Central Carriage Works, Pentre, 1919.

105 The distinctive white Napier car owned by T. R. Evans (centre), Furniture Manufacturer, Retailer and Auctioneer, Ystrad Road, Pentre, *c.*1918.

106 Royal train at Porth Station when King George V opened the Miners' Rescue Station at Dinas,
27 June 1912.

107 Arrival of 5.00 p.m. train, 12 April 1912, Ystrad Station (Taff Vale Railway).

108   Pwll yr Hebog incline engine (Tonypandy to Clydach) built by Kitsons in 1884.

109   "Mountaineer" and "Duty", colliery locomotives in use at Abergorki Colliery, Treorchy, *c*.1890.

110 A 1919 two-cylinder air-cooled eight horse-power Rover car outside Basini's Cafe, Treherbert. Maximum speed 45 m.p.h. Basic price £220, with additional £7 for fitting speedometer, if required.

111 The Timothy family and friends about to set out on a cycling trip. Photograph taken at the entrance to the Timothy Timber Yard, Llanfoist Street, Ton Pentre, *c*.1912.

Entertainment

112 The Rhondda Glee Society, formed 1878, who under their conductor, Tom Stevens, performed at Windsor Castle before Queen Victoria on 22 February 1898.

113 Theatre Royal, Tonypandy, built in 1892. Will Stone's bioscope was introduced in 1910 to supplement the live shows.

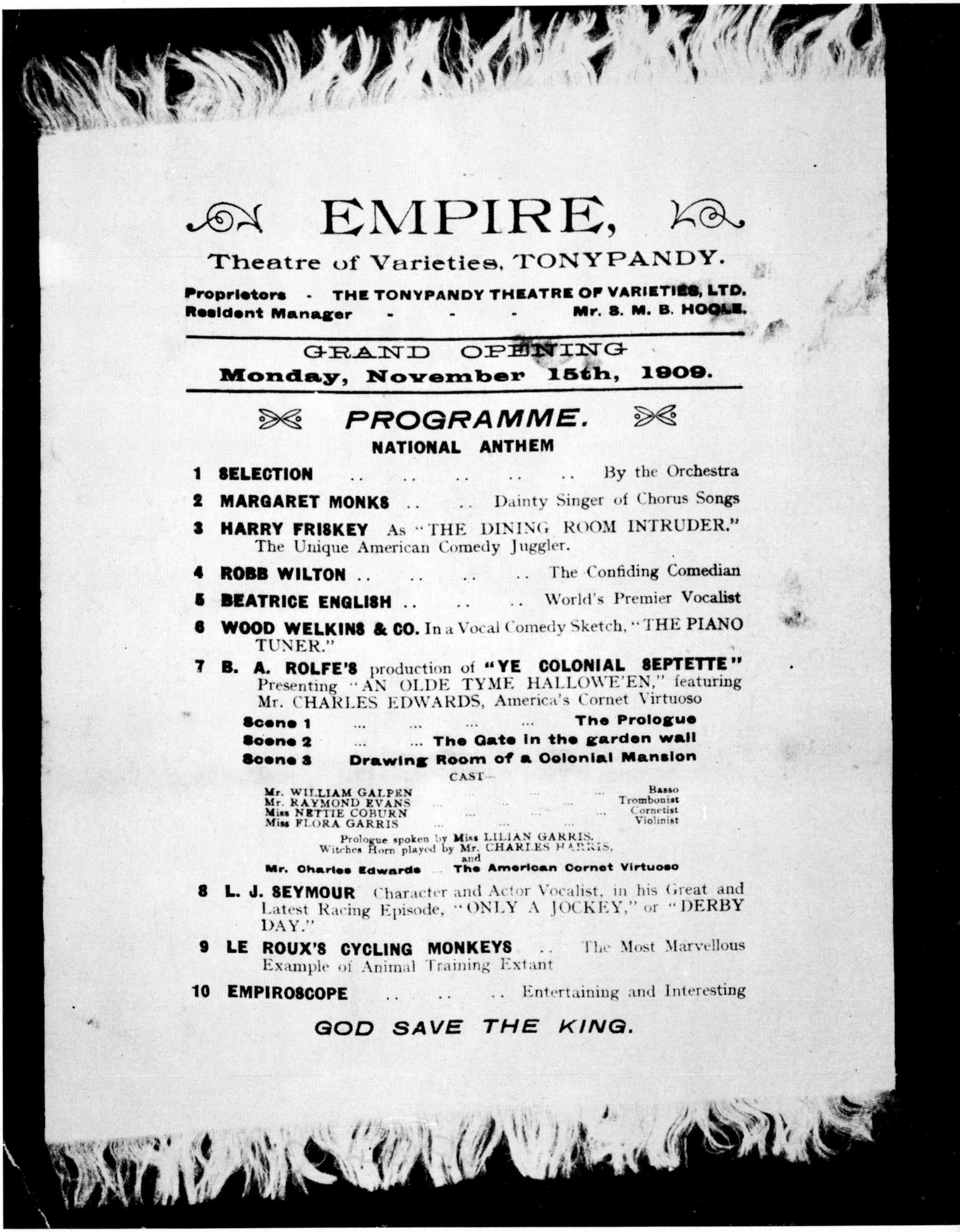

EMPIRE,

Theatre of Varieties, TONYPANDY.

Proprietors - THE TONYPANDY THEATRE OF VARIETIES, LTD.
Resident Manager - - - Mr. S. M. B. HOOLE.

GRAND OPENING
Monday, November 15th, 1909.

PROGRAMME.

NATIONAL ANTHEM

1 SELECTION .. .. By the Orchestra

2 MARGARET MONKS .. .. Dainty Singer of Chorus Songs

3 HARRY FRISKEY As "THE DINING ROOM INTRUDER."
The Unique American Comedy Juggler.

4 ROBB WILTON .. .. The Confiding Comedian

5 BEATRICE ENGLISH .. .. .. World's Premier Vocalist

6 WOOD WELKINS & CO. In a Vocal Comedy Sketch, "THE PIANO
TUNER."

7 B. A. ROLFE'S production of **"YE COLONIAL SEPTETTE"**
Presenting "AN OLDE TYME HALLOWE'EN," featuring
Mr. CHARLES EDWARDS, America's Cornet Virtuoso

    Scene 1 ... ... **The Prologue**
    Scene 2 ... ... **The Gate in the garden wall**
    Scene 3 **Drawing Room of a Colonial Mansion**

CAST—

Mr. WILLIAM GALPEN	Basso
Mr. RAYMOND EVANS	Trombonist
Miss NETTIE COBURN	Cornetist
Miss FLORA GARRIS	Violinist

Prologue spoken by **Miss LILIAN GARRIS.**
Witches Horn played by Mr. CHARLES HARRIS,
and
Mr. Charles Edwards ... **The American Cornet Virtuoso**

8 L. J. SEYMOUR Character and Actor Vocalist, in his Great and
Latest Racing Episode, "ONLY A JOCKEY," or "DERBY
DAY."

9 LE ROUX'S CYCLING MONKEYS .. The Most Marvellous
Example of Animal Training Extant

10 EMPIROSCOPE .. .. .. Entertaining and Interesting

GOD SAVE THE KING.

114 Souvenir programme, printed on silk, to mark the opening of the Empire Theatre of Varieties, Tonypandy, 15 November 1909.

115   Dai Allen (Treherbert) with his portable forge in the parade to celebrate the Relief of Mafeking, May 1900.

116   David Jones, Dowlais Cakes. A float in the parade to celebrate the Relief of Mafeking, passing Ystrad Railway Station.

117 Cory Workmen's Band. Originally formed in 1884 as Ton Pentre Temperance Band, they changed their name after the opening of Gelli Colliery Library in 1895 when Sir Clifford Cory offered to subsidise them and find the band a director of music.

118   Tom Jenkins, Pentre. Featherweight wrestling champion of the world, 1911.

119   The annual Darran Park Horse Show, Ferndale, 1905.

120   Porth Carnival in aid of Porth Cottage Hospital, 1910.

opposite): **121** Joe Slade, founder member of "Ystrad Spuds" later renamed "Ystrad Zulus Carnival Jazz Band", 1926.

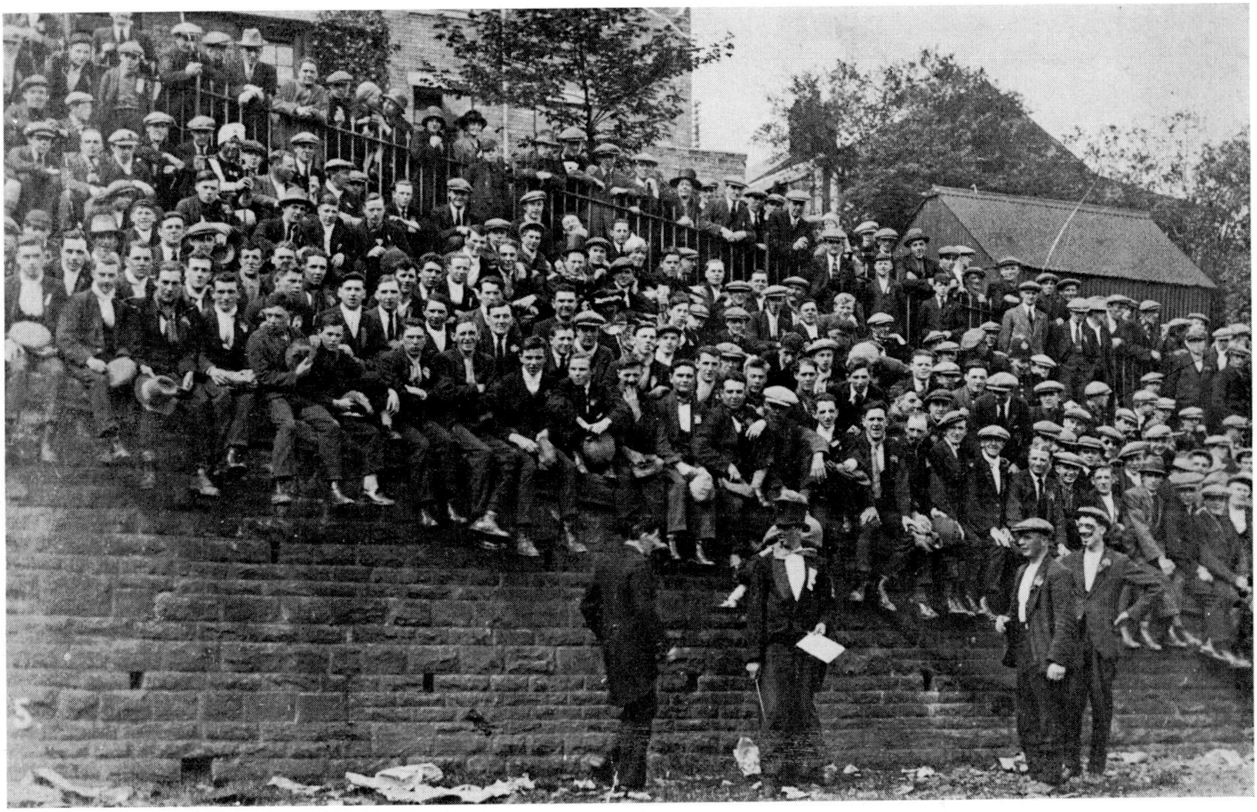

122 Spectators and umpires at a "Catty and Doggy Tournament" at the Oval, Tonypandy, during the General Strike, 1926.

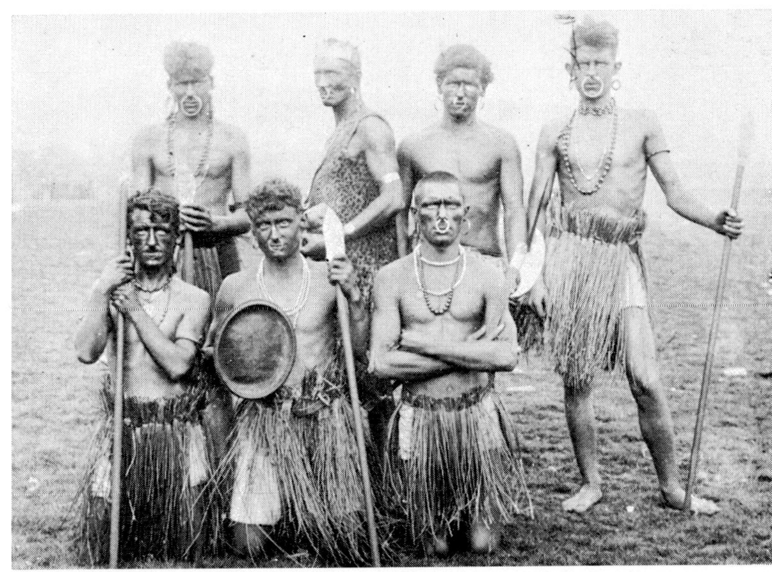

123 Amos Hill's "Penygraig Zulus", 1926.

124 "Gelli Toreadors" whose marching and counter marching, "gazoot" and drum playing, made them one of the most popular bands of 1926.

125 The cast of cantata "Holiday on the Sands", Nazareth Chapel, Blaenllechau, 1919.

Social and Cultural

126 Temperance campaign rally, St. Andrew's Church, Tonypandy. The churches and chapels were most concerned about the dangers of drink and several Temperance Societies were formed from as early as 1865 to combat drunkenness.

127 King George V officially opened the Miners' Rescue Station at Dinas on 27 June 1912. The site chosen is just one hundred yards from the first shaft sunk in the Rhondda.

128 The Royal Party travelled up the Rhondda Fawr to the terminus of the Taff Vale Railway at Treherbert, receiving a tremendous welcome from people who lined the track.

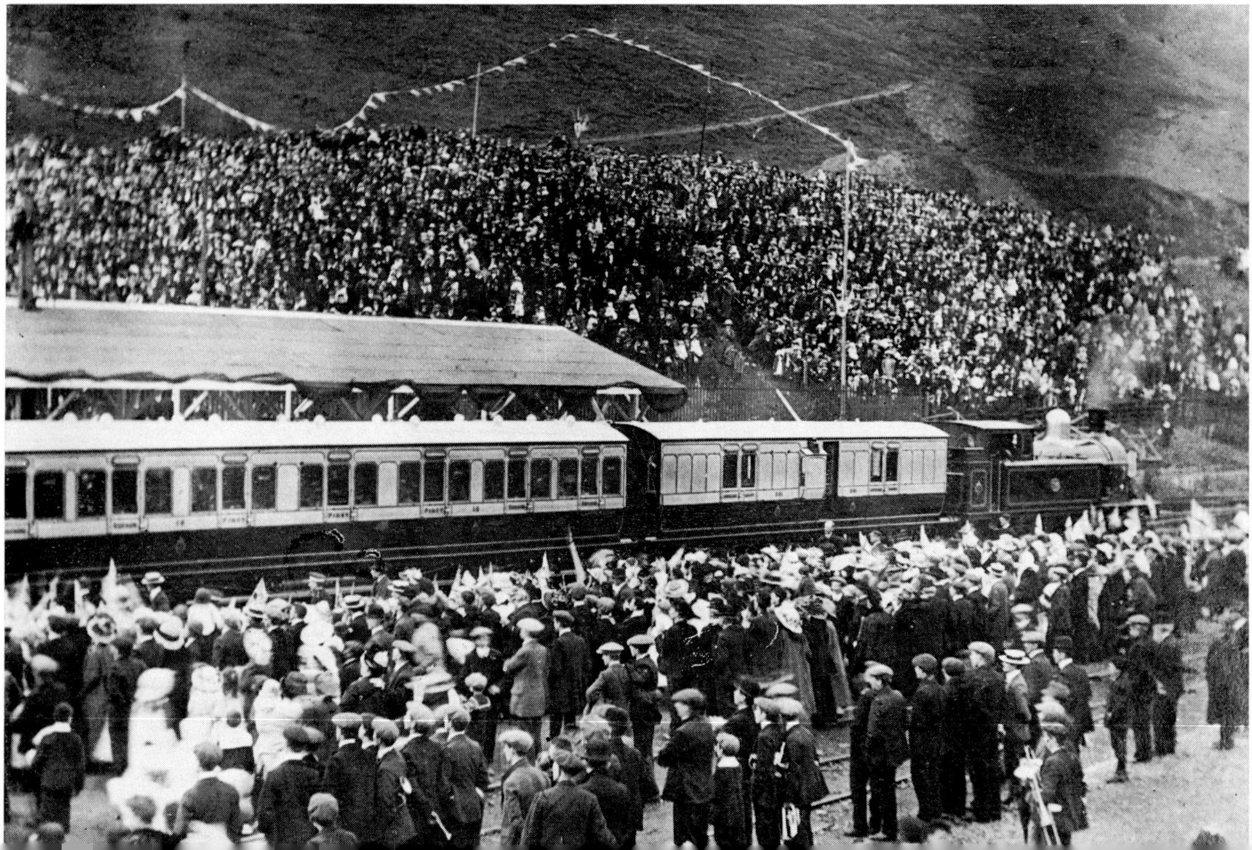

129   Official opening of Glenrhondda Colliery Workmen's Hall and Institute, Blaen y Cwm, April 1924. Institutes provided rooms for meetings and games and most possessed a good library.

130 Statue to Archibald Hood erected in front of the Llwynypia Miners' Library and Institute in 1906. The unveiling ceremony was performed by Rhondda's first M.P., William Abraham (Mabon).

131 With monies left over after the erection of Archibald Hood's statue, a fountain and water trough was erected at Tonypandy Square and unveiled by William Abraham, M.P. (Mabon).

132 Ben Bowen, Treorchy's famous Bard, winner of many eisteddfodau (including London in February 1901). This photograph was taken when he was a guest of the Diamond Fields Cambrian Society, Kimberley, South Africa, in 1902.

133 Unveiling of plaque by W. P. Thomas, J.P., at 126 High Street, Treorchy, birthplace of Ben Bowen. He was born in 1878 and died at the early age of 25, a year after his return from South Africa.

134 Members of the Rhondda Wireless Enthusiasts Society photographed in the grounds of Glyncornel House, Llwynypia, in 1923 (inset, Lt. Col. David Davies, M.P., president). Broadcasting began in Wales on 13 February 1923.

135 The first Poppy Day with a group of sellers outside their headquarters, The Emporium, Ystrad Road, Pentre, selling Flanders Poppies for the Earl Haig Fund, November 1919.

136 "Mabon" arriving home at Ystrad Station, 1918. William Abraham was born in Cwmavon in 1842. He came to the Rhondda in 1877 and was elected to Parliament in 1885. He served as M.P. for Rhondda for 35 years and died in 1922.

137   Pentre Citadel Salvation Army Life Saving Guards, 1925.

138   The 1st Cwmparc pack of Wolf Cubs with Scout Masters George White and Jack O'Brien, 1922.

139 The Spanish competitors in the Gordon-Bennett international balloon race who landed near Fernhill Collieries, Treherbert, 18 September 1921.

140 Walkers in the Church Army route march from Birmingham to Swansea. The Rev. Shilton Evans, then Vicar of St. George's, Cwmparc, and later Rural Dean at Pontypridd, is on the extreme right at the back.

141   The opening of Gelli Park by Councillor Jim James of Ystrad, 1914.

142   Labour Party rally at No. 3 Ton Row, Ton Pentre, 1923. Will John, M.P., is on the extreme
left of the photograph.

143   The Mid Rhondda Orpheus Glee Party on the platform of Tonypandy Railway Station prior to their departure for a London concert, *c.*1912.

144   Tabernacle Wesleyan Sunday School, Dumfries Street, Treorchy, about to start their church walk through Treorchy, *c.*1914.

145 Park and Dare Workmen's Institute, Treorchy. Built in 1894 to provide recreational facilities for workers employed by David Davies, who assisted them with a grant. In 1913 an extension was added which served as a cinema and billiard hall.

146 Bardic ceremony at the Gorsedd, Treorchy, for the National Eisteddfod of 1928.

147 Railway Inn, opposite Ystrad Railway Station, with landlord F. Vokes and Dr. W. E. Thomas outside the entrance, *c.*1910. It was later demolished after a subsidence.

148 Lamb Inn, Ystrad, *c.*1910.

149   Gellidawel Hotel, Ystrad. In 1913 it was demolished and the new Star Hotel built up around it. Throughout the work beer continued to be sold so that the licence could be retained.

150   Tremains Hotel, Cwmparc. Built on the parish road to Nant-y-Moel, near Parc Isaf farm, it was used as a pay office when Parc Pit was sunk in 1865. It was later buried under a coal tip and a new Tremains Hotel was built on Parc Road.

Education and Public Services

151 The staff of Treorchy Board School, 1886. When education became compulsory in 1880 the rapidly expanding population presented a great problem to the Ystradyfodwg School Board. But by 1900 thirty-five schools had been built in the Rhondda.

152   A Cwmparc sewing class, 1898.

153   Ferndale Girls' School, 1914.

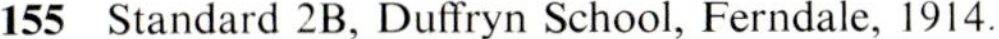

154 King's Scholarship class, Rhondda Pupil-Teachers School, Porth, 1904.

155 Standard 2B, Duffryn School, Ferndale, 1914.

156   Pentwyn Hospital, built in 1924 on the site of Pentwyn Farm to treat and care for accident victims in the local collieries, and financed by subscriptions deducted from miners' wages.

157   Ystradyfodwg Cottage Hospital, Tyntyla, Ystrad, 1887. *Front* seated: Dr. J. R. James, Medical Officer of Health (centre), with the first two patients; *back* the staff, Mr. and Mrs. Aylesbury and maid.

Ystradyfodwg Fire Brigade photographed outside the Council Offices, Pentre, *c*.1890.

159 Ton Pentre Fire Brigade outside Llanfoist Street Fire Station, *c*.1925.

160 James Timothy in the driving seat of a Merryweather fire appliance, Ton Pentre, 1890.

In Sad Remembrance of

63 MEN AND BOYS

WHO WERE

KILLED IN THE MIDDLE PIT,

DINAS COLLIERY, RHONDDA VALLEY,

BY AN EXPLOSION,

On Monday Night, January 13th, 1879.

Of this number there were 46 married and 11 single men, 3 boys under 18, and 3 widowers. The dependent relations are:—46 widows, 130 Children, 2 parents, and 3 sisters.

"DEATH COMES IN ALL SHAPES."

161   This was not the first disaster at Dinas Colliery. Thirty-five years earlier, on 1 January 1844, the first major explosion in the Rhondda occurred with the loss of twelve lives The manager, Daniel Thomas, had a miraculous escape. Together with an apprentice, David Morgan, he was descending the shaft when the explosion took place. The pit-head gear was destroyed and the cage plunged to the bottom. Thomas was injured but recovered; Morgan was less fortunate being one of those killed.

162 Dinas Colliery explosion, January 1879.   The explosion was so fierce that one of the two half-ton iron caps used to seal the mouth of the shaft for ventilation purposes and the steel cage were blown into the wooden framing and hung suspended above the mouth of the shaft.

163 Group photograph of rescuers and rescued in the Tynewydd Colliery inundation of April 1877. Of the rescuers four were awarded the Albert Medal (1st Class) and 21 the Albert Medal (2nd Class), the first time the medal had been awarded for bravery on land.

164 On 11 April 1877 the Tynewydd Colliery, Porth, was inundated with water from the old workings of the nearby Upper Cymmer Colliery. Fourteen men were trapped. Four of these were drowned and one was killed by the rush of compressed air during a rescue attempt. Of the nine survivors four were released after 18 hours and the remaining five after nine days. They are featured in this photograph (*left to right*) John Thomas, George Jenkins, David Hughes (age 15), Moses Powell and David Jenkins.

165 Tynewydd inundation final rescue team. After tunnelling through 38 yards of coal in nine days, working in teams of four, the miners came within rescuing distance of their entombed workmates. This last stage was the most dangerous as they had no means of knowing whether the water level had fallen sufficiently by pumping—if not they would certainly have been drowned. The final onslaught and eventual rescue was made by three friends, Gwilym Thomas, Abraham Dodd and Isaac Pride, on Friday afternoon, 20 April 1877.

166 Tonypandy Square at the time of the Cambrian Strike, November 1910. Trouble began at the Ely Pit, Penygraig, over payment for working the new Bute seam. On 1 September the management locked out all the men employed at Ely, and two months later the South Wales Miners' Federation called out on strike all men—12,000—employed by the Cambrian combine.

167 On 19 December 1910, after a trial which lasted six days, a number of striking Gilfach Goch miners were tried and convicted at Pontypridd of intimidation and assault on a miner they considered a blackleg. The sentences were severe, two miners being sent to prison.

168 Miners involved in the Cambrian Strike opened up coal-levels in the hillside to obtain coal for their own use and to sell to provide sustenance for their families.

169 Skirmishes took place between the police and strikers who were attempting to stop blacklegs working at Glamorgan Colliery. In an encounter at Tonypandy Square on 7 November 1910 windows were broken and some shops looted.

170 Troops of the Lancashire Fusiliers, 218th Hussars and the West Riding Regiment, commanded by General Sir Neville Macready, were posted to the collieries in the Cambrian dispute.

171 Rail disaster at Hopkinstown, 23 January 1911. Eleven passengers were killed. This tragedy came at a time when much misery and suffering were already being experienced due to the Cambrian Strike. The strike dragged on until September 1911 when the men accepted the terms originally offered—2s. 1·3d. per ton for cutting the seam of coal in dispute.

172 Funeral of Councillor Thomas George, Ferndale, one of three members of the miners' executive killed in the above disaster. The others were Councillors William Morgan, Treherbert, and Tom Harries, Pontygwaith.

173 The secret ballot organised by the Union at the pit-head after the day's work was over, decided whether strike action would be taken.

174 Soup kitchens provided a welcome if meagre supplement to the austere diet of the miner's family during times of strike and industrial unrest.

175 A moment of great tragedy. At 11.50 a.m. on Tuesday, 11 July 1905, all but three of the 122 men who went down to work in the 9 ft. seam of the Wattstown No. 2 Pit, including the manager, W. Meredith, were killed.

176 The funeral of victims of the Wattstown disaster. The cortege was reported to extend for five miles. When those at the head of the procession were turning in to Llethr Ddu Cemetery, Trealaw, the last were about to leave Wattstown.

177 The findings of the enquiry into the Wattstown disaster revealed that the explosion was caused by shot firing in a cross heading between the sinking pit and up-cast pit. An attempt was being made to drive a road from the No. 2 pit, where the explosion occurred, to No. 1 pit where a much larger number of men were employed.

178 Mid-Rhondda contingent of miners passing through Bristol on the Hunger March of 1936.

179 The Hunger Marchers singing outside a Leicester Square theatre, London, in order to collect coppers to buy food.

180 Floods at Ystrad, 1910. Subsidence sometimes resulted in valley roads being below the general drainage level. After heavy rain this resulted in impassable roads and disaster for the inhabitants of houses in the flooded areas.

181 Floods at Ynyshir, 1910. In some districts permanent pumping stations were set up so that water could be pumped back into the river.

182/183/184 At 3.45 p.m. on Friday, 11 March 1910, the abandoned "Gwennies" level on the hillside above Clydach, which had filled with water, burst its banks, rushing down the streets, creating havoc in Adam Street, demolishing No. 13, and continuing down Wern Street and into the junior school. It swept some of the children into the yard where the surrounding high stone wall served to dam up the water. The headmaster, R. R. Williams, later Director of Education for Rhondda, and members of his staff succeeded in rescuing many of the children, miners returning from work also helped, but unfortunately three children were drowned in the yard. A lady and six-months-old baby were drowned in Adam Street, and next morning a child who had been playing in the street at the time of the disaster was found drowned in the gutter in Wern Street after the floodwater had subsided.

185 Between August and October 1916 a landslide occurred in Pentre demolishing some shops and a skating rink.

186 Pentre landslide as seen from the Woodfield Hotel, 1916. The threat of severance to the only road linking Tonypandy with Treorchy caused the authorities to think of building subsidiary roads.

187 General view of the Pentre landslide. The much-needed subsidiary roads were built in the 1920s between Ton Pentre and Cwmparc, and Gelli and Llwynypia. Inter-valley roads over the Bwlch and Rhigos were also built, creating improved economic and social possibilities for the future.

188   Before the days of Social Security the families of accident victims had to apply for relief as parish paupers and were given a note to take to an appointed retailer who would supply food to the value indicated.   After the Cymmer explosion of 1856 a widow with three children was allowed 10/- per week, a widow with six children 15/- per week.

189   Strikes resulted from the desperation of miners to improve the appalling conditions of their employment.   Dignity and charity do not go together and it took a lot of resolve to watch your family starve while you sought to obtain a better wage and reasonable conditions.   Life was hard, but was sometimes made a little easier by the generosity of individuals, as in this distribution of buns to the "poor children" by Mr. Gable of the Glandwr Hotel, Ystrad, 5 April 1912.